Paleo Diet

50 Delicious, Pa

Complete Guide To Going Paleo

By Martin Rowland

The trademarks that are used are without any consent, and the publication of the trademark is without permission or backing by the trademark owner. All trademarks and brands within this book are for clarifying purposes only and are the owned by the owners themselves, not affiliated with this document.

Disclaimer – Please read!

The information provided in this book is designed to provide helpful information on the subjects discussed. This book is not meant to be used, nor should it be used, to diagnose or treat any medical condition. For diagnosis or treatment of any medical problem, consult your own physician. The publisher and author are not responsible for any specific health or allergy needs that may require medical supervision and are not liable for any damages or negative consequences from any treatment, action, application or preparation, to any person reading or following the information in this book. References are provided for informational purposes only and do not constitute endorsement of any websites or other sources. Readers should be aware that the websites listed in this book may change.

Table of Contents

What is the Paleo Diet?

For most people, the Paleo concept is new and sparks many questions. After reading this, not only will you know what it is, but how to get in and actually do it. The best teacher is experience and can help you get around the confusion of this way of eating. With all the counterarguments to the Paleo diet out there today, here you will find the true nature of the diet, its benefits, and how to live the Paleo life.

The 'diet' in the Paleo diet misleads people into believing that it is nothing but a temporary weight loss phase. The Paleo diet is based on the belief that in order to achieve optimal health, humans of the modern day should go back to eating real, whole unprocessed foods that are much more healthful, rather than harmful, to our bodies.

As the Paleo diet grew, people adopted the phrase 'the caveman diet,' which makes it seem like another weird fad diet, but trust me, it isn't. For the past 200,000 years, humans have adapted to whole foods: plants, seafood, meat- all of them are full of the nutrients that our bodies evolved to thrive on. Agriculture is a small fraction of our evolutionary history, it came to past a mere 10,000 years ago and there has not been enough time for humans to fully adapt to eating modern foods like sugar, wheat, chemically processed vegetables, seed oils, and other 'Neolithic' foods. With that being said, it should not come as a coincidence to realize that most modern diseases of civilization-including but not limited to autoimmune disorders, type 2 diabetes, cardiovascular disease, and raving obesity-have come with the world-wide spread of industrialized food. This is the sole reason why the Paleo approach breathes heavily on returning to the ancestral approach to eating.

An important thing to keep in mind is that there isn't one monolithic, definitive, 'one-size-fits-all' Paleo diet. Some Paleo eaters may choose to eat super low carbs and others are more easily inclined to eat a baked potato or a bowl of white rice every now and again. In part, there are Paleo eaters who cannot fathom a life without dairy and there are some more orthodox folks who will refuse to touch butter with a 39 1/2 inch pole. The Paleo tent is large enough for many different approaches, but the core of the diet remains the same.

- **Eat whole, unprocessed, nourishing, nutrient-dense foods**

  Make grass fed and pastured eggs and meats, vegetables and wild-caught seafood a priority. Enjoy nuts, seeds, and fruits in moderation.

- **Avoid foods that will harm us in ways of wrecking our guts, systemic inflammation, or off set our natural metabolic processes**

  Abstain from ingesting pro-inflammatory, toxic foods such as grains with gluten in them, laboratory concocted

Franken foods and sugar found in your supermarket. Biochemists, nutritionists, physicians and other researchers are starting to warm up to the idea of ancestral nutrition, and people who take in a Paleo-like approach to eating have reported significant improvements in their state of health, energy levels, and body composition. Even more importantly, there is evidence that the people who eat this way are reducing their risks of various disorders and diseases that are associated with the SAD.

You might be wondering, how can this be healthy? Plenty of people seem to think that adopting the Paleo diet means they have to go super low on their carb intake and how much meat they eat. High quality fats and proteins are part of the equation, but so are vegetables and even, (gasp!) carbohydrates! Yes, you can still eat carbs. It's not like you have to dump all the grains and processed junk off of your plate and replace it with something else. Replace it with fruit and vegetables instead. Substitute the low quality CAFO-raised, steroid injected meat you are accustomed to eating with pastured and grass fed meat, sustainable seafood and eggs. In other words, do your best to avoid lab concocted ingredients and foods that are more likely to be harmful to you than healthful, and prioritize with whole, nutrient packed, real food instead. Follow these three basic rules for optimal benefits:

1. **Follow the Paleo roadmap as clear as possible**

   Yes, you may have occasional setbacks every now and again, some off roading can be enjoyable and worth the indulgence. But you should keep moving in the right direction, which means you have to avoid potholes like soy, gluten, processed junk, and other inflammatory and gut wrecking foods, and added sugars as much as you can.

2. **Simple and quick will do the trick**

   Cooking can become an overwhelming chore when we get really wrapped up in the complicating and time consuming recipes. To be sustainable and practical, ancestral nutrition should be easy.

3. **Last but not least, it better be delicious**

   Way too many people think the Paleo view of eating is based on deprivation. But in reality, they can't see Paleo food as being anywhere close to the tastiness of their scrumptious, everyday meals, or bag of cheese puffs. In order to maintain a Paleo lifestyle, it is important to show them how the food that fuels them can be healthy AND extremely good.

You should also keep in mind that the Paleo diet is not a weight loss cure-all. If years of unhealthy eating have destroyed your metabolism and you are walking around with extra body fat, switching to this diet will definitely help your overall health and body composition. However, the purpose of eating Paleo is not to shed as much weight as you can so you can fit into your old jeans from high school, this nutritional view is about achieving optimal wellness and health-not morphing you into a size zero runway model.

It is best to stick with it for a minimum of 30 days. For a lot of people, switching over to the Paleo diet isn't exactly easy. Because of the sudden drop in carbohydrates, people who are used to mainlining sugar pasta have reported that they feel horrible for the first few weeks, some call it the 'Paleo flu.' If you can make it through this first phase of sluggishness, you will come through feeling great. Also, eat like a champ. Do not be afraid to try new recipes and new foods-including but not limited to healthy dietary fats. The Paleo diet may be very restrictive at first, but if you try to keep an open mind and adventurous appetite, you will soon find that this way of eating can offer flavors, nourishment, and variety.

Health Benefits of the Paleo Diet

You must read these benefits, you need to read it because once you do, and you will realize that the Paleo diet is unquestionably the best diet for you. There is no special pill and you do not have to starve yourself for 40 days and nights. The main problem with your current diet is that you think your body is the best machine in the world and it is invincible. Sorry, it's not. This is why 25% of the American population is suffering from metabolic syndrome...meaning they literally cannot convert food into sustainable energy effectively. The even sadder truth is that many people have been eating in this manner for their entire lives, these people are surviving but they are not thriving. Once you go Paleo, you will see how much better a healthy diet can make you feel. Here are 15 benefits of the Paleo diet.

Healthy Cells- you may not know it, but every cell in your body is made from both unsaturated and saturated fat, and your cells depend on a healthy balance of both in order to keep your body functioning properly. The Paleo diet naturally provides a balance of fats because it allows both in healthy amounts, while other diets limit you to one or the other.

Healthy Brain-one of the best sources of fat and protein suggested by the Paleo diet comes from cold water fish; ideally, wild-caught salmon.

More Muscle, Less Fat-the paleo diet breathes heavily on animal flesh, and healthy protein with it. This protein is highly anabolic and is utilized for building new cells like muscle mass.

The more muscle you have, the better your metabolism will work, no questions asked. This is due to the fact that muscles require energy to move, and in order to move bigger muscles, you have to store energy in them. This will allow your body to send energy to muscle cells instead of the fat cells. By shrinking fat cells and increasing muscle cells through a healthy Paleo diet, any extra energy will be transported to glycogen in your muscles, rather than triglycerides in your fat cells.

Better Gut Health-sugar, processed junk, and other man made fats cause inflammation inside your intestinal tract. Unfortunately, when you match too many processed foods with a lot of stress, you can end up with what's called 'leaky gut syndrome' which is when your intestinal walls are breeched and things that are not supposed to leave end up leaking out.

Circle of Life-the Paleo diet suggests eating pasture raised eggs and meats. This means that the animals are honestly able to roam in grass for the duration of their lives. Most ideally, chickens and cows will roam the pasture with one another as this creates synergy. In nature, chickens follow cows around and eat the bugs and larvae found under the cow pies. The cow pie will be broken up, which fertilizes the grass which in turn will provide food for the cow.

Get all your vitamins and minerals-the Paleo diet also suggests eating the rainbow. Vegetables are a big part of the diet and it is recommended to get a variety of vegetables depending on the seasons. By eating the rainbow you ensure that you get all your vitamins from the different nutrients in the veggies.

Limits Fructose-the Paleo diet recognizes that the human body digests fructose differently than most other carbs. It is for this reason that the Paleo diet suggests strategically choosing and limiting the perfect fruits.

Better digestion and absorption-the Paleo diet suggests eating foods that you have adapted the ability to digest over thousands of years. It is no question as to whether or not you can tolerate starch or grass fed beef, our ancestors survived and thrived off of these foods.

Less Allergies-the Paleo diet suggests that you minimize the foods that are known to be allergens and certain societies. Some people can't digest seeds and dairy, this is why the Paleo diet recommends that you remove these foods from your diet for at least a month. People often bash on the Paleo diet because you can't eat whole grains, and this could not be farther from the truth. The truth is only that grains aren't the best tool for the job, this is why we avoid them from time to time. If you are an athlete, you should probably eat a cup of oats every now and again.

Reduce inflammation-research suggests that inflammation may be the number one factor behind cardiovascular disease. One of the greatest thing about the Paleo diet is that most of the foods are anti-inflammatory so you will be minimizing your risks.

More energy-do you ever wonder whey energy drinks have become so popular in the last ten years? It is because everyone's diet sucks! A normal American breakfast is comprised of a sugar coffee matched with a bagel with cream cheese or a muffin. Not only will this lead to type 2 diabetes at some point and insulin resistance, it won't keep you satiated either.

Weight loss-the Paleo diet is a low carb diet by design. By simply removing processed foods, you will drastically reduce your carb intake and fuel weight loss.

Increased insulin sensitivity-if you ate ice cream with every meal, every day for half a year, I can guarantee that you will start hating ice cream at some point. The same is true for your body, when you fuel your body with sugary, cheap foods constantly, your body desensitizes itself to them because it does not want or need them. Your body only needs so much energy, when you reach that threshold, your cells reject this fuel and store it as fat. If this happens for too long, you will develop insulin sensitivity, meaning your body will not be capable of recognizing when your cells are full or not.

Reduce risk of disease-the Paleo diet is not perfect, but the main focus of it is to avoid foods that could potentially harm your health. The Paleo diet makes it easy to avoid crap foods by providing you with a simple blueprint, only eat what a caveman would be able to eat. This is not perfect but it will make sure you limit your risk for disease by avoiding the foods that have been known to cause them.

Shrink those fat cells-most people do not realize that fat cells shrink and expand depending on your diet. A lean person does not have less fat cells, they simply have smaller ones. In order to keep those fat cells small, you have to choose healthy fats and limit your intake of carbs. Healthy fats are packed tightly together inside your cells and are always available for energy when you are insulin sensitive. There is basic synergy at work here, the Paleo diet naturally provides you with the foods that will add muscle and keep you insulin sensitive, which will make sure your cells stay compact. Avoiding carbs will make sure that your cells stay healthy and able to burn fat.

Have I convinced you to try the Paleo diet? Good.

The Paleo Diet Itself

With all this information, you might need some clarification as to what the Paleo diet actually is. There are two definitive aspects of the diet based on two central ideas: first, humans adapted to eating particular kinds of foods, and in order to stay healthy, fit and strong, and avoid the chronic diseases of our modern day, we need to eat like our ancestors.

Our oldest ancestors, the first primates, lived more than 60 million years ago. And, just like most primates of modernity, they thrived mainly on leaves, insects, and fruits. Around 2.6 million years ago, the dawn of the Paleolithic era, things started to change. These ancestors adapted the opposable thumb and big brains, they started utilizing fire, stone tools, and as a result of this, began to change their diet steadily. As of 50,000 years ago, when the truly modern humans came to part, our ancestors were surviving on an omnivorous hunter-gatherer diet.

With this, we arrive at a basic model of the Paleo diet. This basic plan includes animals: meat, fish, insects, reptiles, etc. - and normally, almost all components of the animals such as bone marrow, organs and cartilage. You may also have animal products such as eggs or honey, leaves, stems, roots/tubers, and stems-in other words, your vegetables. Seeds and nuts can be eaten raw as well. As of today, most Paleo advocates have advised eaters to start with the foods listed above and then slowly present grass fed dairy, like yogurt and some other cultured options, and small portions of legumes that have soaked overnight.

Paleo is a branch, or a more complex and modern version of the diet of a hunter-gatherer. Around 10,000 years ago, most of civilization discovered agriculture, thus moving us from the Paleolithic period to the Neolithic period. Farming and planting have provided us with a consistent and somehow reliable food supply, which civilization could have never developed. A large number of people believe that the transition from a hunting and gathering diet, heavy in vegetables and wild fruits, to an agricultural diet, heavy in cereal grains, is what gave way to the chronic diseases of modernity like diabetes, cardiovascular disease and obesity. This is a fundamental part of the Paleo diet and a large reason why some people believe we should retreat back to the produce and meat-based diet of our earliest days.

Ancestral eaters fare relatively well, yes, we have extensive skeletal remains, cooking sites and some other kinds of evidence, but we do not have the intricate medical records of our hunter-gatherer ancestors. But, we do have real sample populations to examine. The very small number of hunter-gatherer populations that are still thriving survive on a very wide variety of diets from the 'seedy and nutty' African Kung, to the Kitavans that eat root-vegetables, and the fat and meat-loving Inuits of the Artic.

These foraging diets are very diverse and in all likelihood reflect the broadly varying diets of our prehistoric ancestors because what people ate relied directly on where they lived. In the tropics, their diet will be mostly plant based, and in the artic, they will be mostly animal-based, along with everything in-between. No matter how varied their diets were, most Paleolithic humans probably consumed around three times more produce than the average American. When you compare this to the typical American of today, Paleolithic humans ingested more protein, fiber, unsaturated fat, omega-3 fatty acids, minerals and vitamins, less saturated fat and less sodium.

The main idea of this primal diet, as you may probably have collected, is that our ancient human generic modeling does not match the current diet and lifestyle of the 21st century. As a result, our health and well-being suffer. The Paleo diet also makes some important evolutionary premises:

- Paleolithic hunter-gatherers were healthy and robust, if they did not die young from diseases or accidents, then they lived around as long as we do now.
- When Paleolithic hunter gatherers shifted to Neolithic agriculture, they became relatively, spindlier, shorter, and sicker.
- Modern hunter-gatherers are healthy and their hearth dwindles when they transition to a more modern diet.

With all this in mind, it is important to remember that there is no single Paleo diet. Our ancestors pretty much lived all over the world and in extremely diverse environments, while eating incredibly varied diets. But still, in most cases, primal diets definitely included more fruits and vegetables than most people normally eat today. If we want to be healthier, then we should do what our ancestors did and eat more of those. This may be a valid approach but not necessarily for the recommended Paleo proponents. First and foremost, most modern vegetables and fruits are not like the ones eaten by our ancestors. The earliest fruits and vegetables were often much smaller, bitter, sometimes even toxic, and harder to harvest. As time went on, we started breeding plants with more enticing and preferable traits, along the lines of the sweetest flesh, prettiest colors, fewest natural toxins, largest yields, and biggest fruits. We also diversified types of plants by creating new cultivars from similar origins, like hundreds of tomatoes or potatoes from a few ancestral varieties. Along the same lines, most modern animal foods are not the same either. Beef steak, even if it is grass fed, is not the same as deer meat or bison steak. This does not make modern meat or modern produce appear bad or good, it is merely different from most everything that was accessible in Paleolithic times. The claim that we should eat a diet that is rich in fruits, meats and vegetables arose because we have evolved to eating those specific foods is a bit suspect. The ones that we eat today did not even exist in the Paleolithic era.

Advocates of the Paleo diet argue to the idea that our ancestors' diets could in no way have included a lot of legumes, dairy foods or grains. They also contend that the previous 10,000 years of agriculture is not enough time to adapt to these 'new' foods.

Grains are not the only plant type that the Paleo diet limits. Proponents of the diet also suggest that you avoid eating legumes-peanuts, lentils, peas and beans for a similar reason. But, the belief that legumes were not available abroad or eaten in Paleolithic times is false. A review in 2009 revealed that our

Paleolithic ancestors did not just eat legumes, they were a very important part of their diet.

Another view on the Paleo diet is that ingesting grains can leave you with inflammation and other related health problems. This may be true for people with celiac disease and for people with non-celiac gluten sensitivity, but the research does not support this argument. Observational research has hinted that whole grains may decrease inflammation while refined grains may increase inflammation. Processing could cause problems, not the grain, and eating grains, whether they be whole or defined, does not have any effect on inflammation at all. A reliable body of proof from both controlled and observational research implies that eating whole grains improves aspects of our health such as:

- Improved blood lipids
- Less inflammation
- Better blood glucose control
- Lower risk of coronary heart disease and stroke
  The Paleo diet gets plenty of things right:
- Paleo eating breathes heavily on lean proteins, healthy fats, seeds, fruits, nuts, whole foods, and vegetables
- Paleo eating increases our awareness of how crappy and processed most of our 21st century food is
- Paleo eating has been very effective for improving many chronic diseases.

Summary: What Is the Paleo Diet?

When starting the Paleo diet, you should be very strict for the first thirty days. During this period, you may find that you have relieved certain allergies you didn't know you had, and your body may have been intolerant to certain foods as well.

Stay away from genetically modified foods and stay natural. The sole purpose of the diet is to return to the most natural ways of eating, the diet of the Paleolithic era.

It is also important to consider the positive things about ancestral lifestyles. This can include fresh food, lots of movements, fresh air, a strong social network and good sleep. Think about your place on the spectrum, from processed 21st century food and life to choices that are more in tune with what your body loves and needs. You should take this opportunity to learn more about your ancestors and keep it sane and simple. Doing a few things very well is a lot better than trying to get a lot of things perfect, like eating fresh vegetables and getting a little extra sleep. Most importantly, you should stay informed and critical. Avoid all cultish and dogmatic thinking, look for evidence and be skeptical. You have to question everything, primal eating is a great idea and can turn out to be just what you need, just keep your brain in the game.

We all know that the fitness and health world can sometimes be a very confusing place, but this is not what it has to be. Most

Paleo advocates encourage and appreciate the moderate amounts of starch, as well as dark chocolate, non-grain spirits and red wine being added to your diet. These additions make life a lot more pleasant and it makes eating healthy more achievable and attractive. In the end, sanity, personal preferences, and moderation take priority over any specific food list, evolutionary theory or anti nutrient avoidance.

People who eat Paleo eat a lot more protein when compared to other diets. An abundance of protein helps our lean mass remain dense and strong, keeps us satisfied by our meals and keeps us lean. The Paleo diet may in fact be the best plan, but it is hard to know this for sure without direct comparisons that match calories and macronutrients.

The complex, dynamic, and diverse nature of our microbiome helps explain why some people tend to do well on one type of diet while others will perform and feel better with another type, despite the fact that we are all 99% genetically the same. With further reading, you can understand the Paleo diet to a greater complexity, and learn how to implement it on your own.

Implementing the Paleo Diet

The Paleo diet, in its most basic form, is eating like a caveman used to. You eat anything a caveman could hunt or find-fish, nuts, meats, seeds, regional vegetables and leafy greens. The pasts, candy and cereal has to go. I as much as any other person hates counting calories, it is hard to keep track of how much you have eaten, and it is a nuisance to obsess over it. Fortunately, if you broaden your horizons and get rid of specific kinds of foods from your diet, then you can stop worrying about having to count calories.

Dr. Loren Cordain, a member of the faculty of the Department of health and Exercise Science at CSU, and the author of 'The Paleo Diet' has created, with other colleagues, the Paleo Diet. In its simplest form, it is based on eating contemporary, wholesome foods from the food groups that are similar to the ones of our hunter-gatherer ancestors, and is what they thrived on. Paleo includes fresh meats, more preferably grass produced or free rage game meat, lamb, poultry, beef, pork, fresh fruits, seafood, nuts, seeds, vegetables and healthy oils like coconut, olive, macadamia, flaxseed, walnut and avocado oil.

To better understand the phenomenon that is the Paleo diet, here is a 'who, what, where, when and why' of how the Paleo diet works. It does not have to be an all-or-nothing thing but proponents of the diet testify that the best results can only be reached if you commit to the process with a whole heart.

The What

The Paleo diet encourages eaters to eat only in the way nature intended us to, or the way our ancestors ate in the Paleolithic era before processed foods and grains were introduced to our diets. There is a belief that our bodies evolved from the basis of what our ancestors ate before the rise of agriculture, evidence from archeologists shows that hunter-gatherers tended to be healthier than the agriculturalists. The bones of our ancestors do not show any evidence of the same level of diseases that are found in the remains of agricultural peoples. Because our ancestors thrived off whole, real foods like vegetables, seeds, nuts, and lean meats, the Paleo approach encourages the mirroring of that lifestyle. Advocates of the Paleo diet argue that our present diet has only been so for the past 10,000 years, and it is the SAD that revolves around very large amounts of carbohydrates, refined sugar and other processed foods that are to blame for the unhealthy food regimes that people of today suffer from poor health from, yet still sustain. The Paleo regime is a diet that some people take part in for physical performance, while others do it for weight loss purposes. Whatever the case may be, the theory of the diet is that you can eat like a caveman and get rid of unwanted weight without tediously counting calories. Eating like our prehistoric ancestors will make us leaner and less prone to heart disease, diabetes, other health problems and cancer. The high fiber, high protein eating plan is also referred to as the Caveman diet or the Stone Age Diet.

The Who and the Where

Next is the 'who' behind the Paleo diet, plenty of onlookers are quick to associate this diets lifestyle with their friends who do crossfit, and there is a reason behind this. A trusted website, Livestrong.com, states that the majority of crossfit coaches push their athletes to start following the Paleo regimens because the approach of eating matches the dietary guidelines of the crossfit exercise programs.

Crossfit athletes believe that the Paleo diet brings them to their best athletic performance, similar to the Zone diet which crossfit pushed originally, Paleo supports a specific ratio of protein, fats, and carbs, and is also pretty easy to follow. Crossfit athletes also believe that Paleo heightens performance because, in the opinion of Fitbie, muscle growth is triggered by branch chain amino acids, and lean proteins are a reliable source of them whilst grains are a poor one. While on the Paleo diet, consumers eat more meat and eliminate grains, this way they can get more muscle building protein.

The Paleo diet adds to the 'culty', tribal mentality of crossfit. Crossfit athletes want to feel like they are part of something, nearly counter-cultural with both their exercise and eating habits, the atypical Paleo diet advocates those intentions and distinguishes them from the crowd.

While this diet is common among crossfit athletes, non-crossfit athletes participate in this regimen of eating too-and plenty of people support the idea that Paleo does more than stimulate muscle building, but also helps you get rid of unwanted weight. Non-crossfit athletes who decide to eat Paleo are generally inclined to back away from processed foods that have certain preservatives, sugars and salts. Following the Paleo diet does not promise that consumers are making good food choices, but it does make it more difficult to give way to the processed food that plenty of people love and health professionals love to hate.

The How

This is the tricky part; actually keeping up with the dietary plan of the Paleo diet. Plausibly, the Paleo diet is better defined by what you are not supposed to eat rather than what you are allowed to eat. As mentioned before, Paleo dieters cannot eat any foods that are processed meaning no dairy, refined vegetable oils, wheat and salts. They can, however, eat lean meats and vegetables, fish, seeds, nuts, and eggs, and natural oils such as avocado, coconut and olive oil. Navigating through the Paleo regulations and rules might sound like it is complex but a good thing to keep in mind is that if the food is presented in some kind of cute packaging, then it is probably not Paleo.

And do not forget that Paleo necessitates no dairy and wheat. Most consumers forget that these foods are processed. With this in mind, go for the vegetables and meat rather than the dairy and bread.

As for the crossfit athletes that follow Paleo, the program incentivizes people to follow an objective where calories should be separated into 30% of protein, 30% of fat and 40% of carbohydrates. Paleo strategies also advocate trying the diet for a minimum of 30 days to see how the body reacts, this is branded as the 'Whole 30,' where dieters are encouraged to stay strict with the diet, and this trial run leaves some room for cheating. When eaters are just starting out, they are allowed three cheat meals per week but eventually, those are taken away.

The Why

Paleo supporters get a lot of bother because a handful of experts state that the diet encourages consumption of fat in excessive amounts. But the diet's supporters disagree, especially the crossfit athletes. They believe that the preferred source of energy for our bodies is fat due to the fact that it is a fuel that burns much slower, and is thus the most efficient source of energy for our body to use. Paleo eaters agree, however, that fat gets a bad reputation because too many humans eat carbohydrates in excess, which is why our bodies burn the carbs rather than the fat, leaving us with excess amounts of fat that is stored for later use. But by reducing how many cheap carbohydrates we eat, the Paleo diet lets the body start burning the fat.

The Paleo diet does permit the ingestion of some carbs but supporters argue that followers should not eat simple carbohydrates such as pasta and white bread simply because these simple carbs break into sugar faster and inhibit an insulin response that keeps the body's insulin levels elevated. When insulin levels are high, the body is kept from lipolysis, the process of burning fat. In other ways, complex carbs, the sort that the Paleo diet supports, requires a longer time to break down which in turn will not heighten insulin levels as fast as simple carbs do. Most people forget that Paleo rules apply to drinks too. Paleo eaters are prescribed to spring or filtered water, coconut water, herbal tea, and freshly juiced vegetables and fruits for the same reasons.

The When

When is eating Paleo a good idea? Some people will say all the time and others will say never, it varies. Now that you have a broken down understanding of the diet, you can choose for yourself whether or not you support the regime, but health professionals have differing views. People in the pro Paleo group stay with the logic mentioned before and the arguments behind the diet, while those who are against make quite a few different claims. One claim, shed light on by Scientific

American, claims that humans are not biologically identical to our predecessors from the Paleolithic era, neither do we have access to the same foods that they eat, therefore, following their dietary plan is illogical.

Evolutionary biologist Marlene Zuk claims that the Paleo diet fails to consider that through our evolution, we inherited many adaptations from our Paleolithic ancestors, and we are not uniform with our Stone Age humans. With this in mind, not taking advantage of our modernized ways of eating simply does not make sense. If other organisms and humans could only thrive in situations similar to the ones their ancestors lived in, then life would not have lasted all that long.

For the nutritious side of things, dieticians believe that removing many food groups like grains and dairy is not nutritionally correct because these groups provide us with essential nutrients like vitamin D, calcium, magnesium, antioxidants in grains, phosphorous in dairy and fiber.

Following the Paleo diet makes it too simple to choose certain meats that have high levels of bad cholesterol and LDL saturated fat. Eaters take out dairy while on the diet, meaning they are not getting fat from dairy anymore, but some of the forbidden foods for Paleo eaters, such as brans, whole grain oats, and other legume and grain sources of fiber have been proven to moderate cholesterol levels. Without them, eaters will be at risk.

There you have it: the Paleo diet and widely known arguments from both anti and pro groups. You now understand the logic behind the diet and can further understand all the aspects of it. You no longer have to be confused when you see your crossfit friends eating vegetables and meat for breakfast, lunch, and dinner.

Starting the Diet

One of the most important things to remember about the Paleo diet is that first, it is not a diet per say, it is an entirely new way of looking at food, and it is a lifestyle change. Meaning, it should not be temporary. Paleo focuses on eating nutrient-dense, unprocessed, whole foods that your body can easily digest and use to perform most efficiently.

The main things you are supposed to eat on paleo include meats, vegetables, seeds, nuts and fruits. Foods that you should not eat are sugars, legumes, dairy, grains and processed foods.

The most important step in any transition is getting started, but it is also the hardest. With these steps, you can begin your transition into a healthy Paleo lifestyle.

Step 1: Execute a Kitchen Makeover

It may be nice to think that you have all the restraint in the world and you can withstand all and any temptation, specifically when it comes to food, but in all honesty, you can't. Willpower is not a renewable resource and can actually deplete throughout the struggles of the day. This is a possible reason why a lot of us have a difficult time staying true to our nutrition plans by the days end or over a weekend.

If you have unhealthy food at your house, chances are it will be eaten eventually. Unhealthy foods are more than often easier and take less time to prepare than healthier foods, so when we are hungry, we go right for the potato chips instead of chopping up and cooking some vegetables. The only solution is to make it hard to do the bad stuff, and easier to do the good stuff. You do this by getting rid of all the temptations, the best way is by re-doing your kitchen. Out with the bad, and in with the good.

Black bagging it is an easier concept, you want to take out all of the junk that is crowding your kitchen and replace it with foods from the aforementioned list that form the Paleo diet. In your pantry, look for items like these:

    a. Pretzels

    b. Granola bars

    c. Pretzels

d. Crackers

e. Chocolate

f. Breads/pasta/bagels

g. Candy

h. Cereal

i. Baked goods

j. Flavored nuts

k. Instant foods

In your freezer, look for these items:

a. Waffles

b. Ice cream

c. Chocolate/candy

d. Frozen dinners

e. Cookie dough

f. Hot dogs

In the fridge, look for these items:

a. Cream cheese

b. Milk

c. Condiments

d. Fruit juice

e. Peanut butter

f. Alcohol

g. Breads, whole grains, bagels

h. Caloric beverages

i. Margarine

j. Anything sweetened

k. Leftovers from restaurants

l. Processed meats

These lists do not have everything, but they provide you with a generic idea. If it came in a bag, wrapper, or box, throw it out. If it exceeds three ingredients, throw it out. If some of the ingredients are unpronounceable, throw it out. And if you are not certain about a specific food, just be safe and throw it out. Do not think this is wasting food, these foods are bad and inhibit disease and an unhealthy lifestyle, do not feel bad, instead feel liberated when throwing this crap out.

Step 2: Go grocery shopping

An empty kitchen won't help you eat right, now that all the bad food is gone, it's time to hit your local Trader Joe's, Whole Foods, sprouts, or any grocery store and start shopping. You should be sure to learn to read a label as well. In fact, the food you should be buying should not have a food label, but if it does, this is a good rule:

- No ingredients-this is perfect
- One ingredient- this is good
- Two ingredients- not as good, but still okay
- Three ingredients- this is pushing the limit
- Four or more ingredients-don't get it
  Another tip; not everything needs to be organic.

Step 3: Learn to Cook

Don't laugh, this is important. You have cleared out your kitchen and found the right groceries, what's next? For some, the idea of having to cook may be a bit terrifying but you don't need to serve it up like Rachel Ray or Bobby Flay in order to make healthy, Paleo meals.

Your plate should be a majority of vegetables, with animal protein occupying the space of about 1 or 2 palms depending on your level of activity. How much cooking oil you use will change as well- about 1-4 tablespoons, depending on your gender and size. You should focus on using oils that become solid at room temperature, coconut oil for example, because they fare much better under heat than do liquid fats. You can use olive oil too, just at a lower heat.

Chew fully, eat slowly and only eat to satiety. You should not count calories or weigh food anymore.

Quick tip; do not get too consumed with making difficult and long recipes at the start. Is it a lot easier to maintain healthy eating habits if you make the cooking process simpler. Recipes can be time consuming and difficult sometimes so choose about 5 or 6 recipes, master them and eat them until you just can't stand them anymore before learning a new batch of recipes. It will help to find a reliable Paleo cookbook, or stay tuned for some listed here.

Step 4: Exercise

You knew it was coming, you have to be active to be completely healthy. Cavemen and women spent a large amount of their days on their feet, whether they were sprinting from predators, mixing in bouts, and chasing prey or lifting heavy things and walking from place to place to find a place to sleep.

Fitness does not have to be made complicated either. You can start out with body weight exercises to build up your endurance and strength, and increase your level of fat loss.

Quick tip; learn how to become more active by doing things different in your daily routine. Park farther away in the parking lot, take the stairs and jog when going to get the mail. Find more time for play by participating in recreational leagues or sports, or by going on some walks with family and friends.

Step 5: Sleep

Sleep is of vital importance to initiating perfect paleo wellness and health. You will need plenty of sleep in order to aid your body's recovery from the daily grind and exercise. There are many benefits from healthy sleeping habits that stretch wide and far, including:

- Better performance for athletes
- Decreased risk of heart disease, type 2 diabetes, obesity

- Increased energy
- Enhanced mental focus and memory
- Improved attitude and mood
- Higher tolerance for stress
- Stronger immune system

With these tips, you can start getting a better night's sleep:

- **Turn the TV Off.** The noise and light interferes with the deep, rejuvenating level of sleep that you need for ultimate energy and health. Cavemen did not have TV's, they had concealed caves.

- **Make use of dark curtains and blinds.** This is for when street lights and lamps illuminate your bedroom at night.

- **Shut off the computer.** Turn off all the monitors, and even cover the alarm clock up. You want your room to be as pitch black as a caveman's cave was.

- **Sleep in a cool place.** If you have ever wondered why we love the a/c when it gets warm, this is why. When our bodies are too warm or hot, it is harder for us to focus or relax. If too much heat or warmth causes you some discomfort throughout the day, just think about what would happen when you are sleeping. Your sleep is extremely disrupted when you are too hot or warm. In fact, people have complained about an inability to sleep when it is too warm. No, your room does not have to be as cold as the North Pole but you do want it to be cold enough to maximize sleep.

- **Try getting to bed and waking up at uniform times.** Getting onto a systematic sleep schedule will do wonders for you. Your body will start getting tired and waking up without any effort because of the consistency.

Some things to look out for

When transitioning to the Paleo lifestyle, the first 14 days may be a little bit difficult. As your body is starting to cleanse itself, release toxins, and transform into a fat burner rather than a sugar burner, you might encounter a few side effects like sugar cravings and fatigue. Here are 30 things you will encounter in the first 30 days of the Paleo diet:

1. **Do not expect a miracle the first 3 days.** Do not even expect to be in a good mood. You will be experiencing withdrawal symptoms from carbs and feel lethargic, you may think that it is

not worth it. Do whatever you have to do, cry if you need to, but just push through it.

2. **Your body will detox the first week** and you will start flushing out-do not be worried about the frequent trips to the bathroom. Your body will start reacting unusually to the increased consumption of fat, but don't be scared, this is only temporary. You may find it hard to crush cravings, but you just have to say no. every day that you make it without slipping off the wagon, the easier it gets and the stronger your willpower will get.

3. **You will not feel like exercising** at all for the first 14 days so just do what you can.

4. **You will start to analyze food labels** and then discover that if it has a label, you should not be eating it. Your shopping trips will be shorter and more expensive but it is worth it. Skim the outside of the grocery store for fish and meat supplies and fresh groceries. You

only need to go down the middle aisles for the herbs, spices, and oils.

5. **As you start the third and fourth weeks** your levels of energy will start returning to normal, in fact, you will start to feel what will be amazing-constant energy.

6. **Your emotions will stabilize-**you might feel relatively happy, all the time.

7. **Coconuts are a gift.** The milk is delicious, both for cooking and drinking, even in coffee. It is a great snack and the oil makes everything taste good, even to eat off a spoon for snack especially if you have a binging tendency, it kills off craving. It also makes your skin, nails, and hair luxurious.

8. **You learn to love fat-** it adds flavor and texture and can keep you full for hours. Plus, it is a good energy source.

9. **Your stomach does not have any meal/time constraints-** you can eat when you are hungry and you stop when you are full. All the fat and protein normally means that you do not

feel like snacking and you don't have to eat on a clock.

10. **All cravings for everything sugary, overly process or artificial will disappear-** you may feel uncomfortable for about a week as you actively control what you eat but soon it will become second nature. Those chips or ice cream that you once craved will start to look more like a few days of intestinal discomfort and close distance to the bathroom.

11. **You will be a whiz in the kitchen-** the natural and fresh foods you have to eat will mean more time for meal prep and planning, but your kitchen performance will improve exponentially and you will have fun turning old Paleolithic recipes into Paleo feasts.

12. **You will never be bloated.** Ladies, not even at that time of the month, and for anyone ever.

13. **You do not have to give up your social life.** Caveman liked to look for

pleasure too and they may have even partied too.

14. **You will find that you can make any meal at a restaurant Paleo-friendly** if you just swap out a few sides and ask to hold the dressing.

15. **Weird smells?** If you have gone very low carb and use fish oil supplements, then you will find some body odor changes and your breath may start to smell, try chewing on peppermint leaves.

16. **Consume a lot of water.** The extra protein demands more water in order for your body to wash out all the waste and toxins. With a low carb diet, you will need a lot more water to stay hydrated and keep your mouth from drying out.

17. **Sleep.** Everything else is not worth the effort if you don't sleep. If you do it right, then you should be sleeping like a log and then be able to wake up without an alarm clock.

18. **If you go VLC, very low carbs, your sleep may be disrupted due**

to increased insulin levels. Try taking magnesium and vitamin D before you go to bed. You may even have lucid dreams.

19. **Expect blemished skin to clear up.** Your hair will be shinier, your eyes will brighten and you will have an all-around glowing feeling.

20. **You are not fit.** This may be true, many advocates believe that crossfit is the true test of your fitness levels while on the Paleo diet.

21. **Forget having a pain free body.** If you start doing crossfit, it will force you to work hard and max out every time you work out.

22. **You may feel heavy after a meal of protein.** You might feel like you have put on a few pounds, but you haven't. You can eat less and still have the same satiety feeling, whilst your meals are denser in calories, you are still losing weight. But, you should forget about the scales, use measurements to judge and how your

clothes fit. You should also keep track of your physical performance.

23. Schedule more time for exercise and sleep. You also need to fit in time for socializing, the Paleo and crossfit communities are supportive so you are bound to make a few new friends.

24. New phrases will come about like 'I can't, I have crossfit,' and 'is it Paleo?'

25. Nearly everything the media has said about nutrition and health is false- besides teaching your body a new way to exist, the Paleo and crossfit world will be a challenge for you mentally. You will learn to challenge widely accepted social ideals and will enter an entirely new league of fitness and health knowledge.

26. You learn to handle a lot of things- you will receive many confused stares and miss-informed abuse, along with questions from the ignorant, intrigued and informed. People are easily threatened by what they do not know and some believe that it is a fad while some say it is just crap, just be ready to tell other people your choices and be welcoming to a variety of responses.

27. **Don't excuse the choices you make-** you should not have to make up false illnesses to account for your new lifestyle.

28. **Days 29-30-** you will not regret the day you chose to start, and it only gets better from here.

You might get some grief from friends and family members about your new habits of eating. Just keep in mind that change can be scary and when you change, you change things for others as well. Here are some things to remember when talking to friends and family members about your new lifestyle.

1. Mention what you can and cannot eat- when you tell people that you aren't allowed to eat a certain food, they might get a bit defensive seeing as they are eating these foods. It can come off like you are ridiculing

them for deciding to eat differently than you.

2. Let the results talk for you. It is plain and simple, paleo works and it does wonders. When the fat starts to melt away and your energy levels are through the roof, everyone will be asking how you do it.

3. Keep yourself educated. There are plenty of great resources available to learn from about the Paleo diet. Keep learning, so when interested people start asking you about it, you are properly informed with real facts that they can apply.

    The first step to adopting the Paleo diet is merely getting started. The right time is right now- you can do a kitchen makeover in a few minutes and head to the grocery store, then cook a meal within a few hours. So why wait?

15 Tips for Success

These few tips can get you on the road to perfect Paleo, reference these to stay on track with your new lifestyle.

Step 1: sleep. 8-10 hours every night is the best, odd hours like 3am to 1pm do not count. Try to go to bed at a decent time. The more active you are, and the higher stress levels your lifestyle provides, the more rest you will need. Sleep helps you with food cravings, performance, stress, disease prevention and your mood.

Step 2: get rid of sugar, it literally takes away all the nutrients from your body and causes dramatic spikes in your blood sugar levels and can cause energy crashes as well as promote diabetes and fat storage. Avoid table sugar, artificial sweeteners and fruit juices. Check labels and ingredients for added sugars, this includes dried fruit as well.

Step 3: beans, wheat, peanuts, rye, soy, barley, and quinoa. Oats, brown rice and corn would be no-no's. Whole grain only means a whole 'lotta problems. Most grains have gluten in them which can damage the lining of your gut and steals the vitamins and minerals that our body needs. Go for vegetables or tubers like taro or sweet potato instead.

Step 4: eliminate industrial seed oils. Corn, peanuts, canola, vegetables, soybean, sunflower, and sallflower are some but not all of them. Stay away from hydrogenated and partially hydrogenated oils too. These are found in fake butter spreads and are in most prepackaged foods. Canned nuts normally have them and most restaurants have them as well.

Step 5: go for meals rather than snacks. 3 or 4 meals at an evenly spaced out manner will be best, about every 4 hours. Eat when you are hungry and do not stress out if you skip a meal. Really focus on the quality of your meals.

Step 6: grass fed, local, pasture raised and organic foods contain lower levels of antibiotics and hormones, and also have better omega-3 to omega-6 ratios. Farmers markets provide a great opportunity to talk with farmers about how the animals are raised, treated and cared for. If you cannot buy meats this way then look for the leanest cuts you can get and cook them with healthy fats like coconut oil.

Step 7: get outside, take a break from your daily chores and errands to spend a minimum of 30 minutes outside every day. Expose your neck, arms and face. Regular exposure to the sun will help you get the vitamin D that you need and fight disease and fatigue.

Step 8: exercise right, keep it short and intense but make sure to get some variety. Long, slow hikes, weight training, tai-chi and yoga are great ways to combine aerobics, flexibility and strength. Listen to your body and rest when it is time to.

Step 9: exclude dairy, most dairy produced has a lot off hormones and antibiotics. Vegetables provide lots of calcium so you do not need to worry about that, if you just can't seem to live without it, choose local, full-fat, raw and grass fed choices, goat milk is a good choice.

Step 10: eat a rainbow, choose a wide variety with a lot of color. Highlight leafy and green but shop for color to get additional nutrients. Cook with healthy fats like coconut oil and use it in salads, top those with avocado oil or olive oil.

Step 11: go easy on the nuts and fruits. 1 to 2 servings of fruits, about a handful, and 1 to 2 small handfuls of nuts a day should be okay for you. Both of them are easy to over eat and can give you digestive problems. The fructose in fruit can slow down fat loss and interrupt thyroid, so choose low sugar options such as different berries and stay away from tropical fruit, they are higher in sugar like mangos and papayas.

Step 12: do less of what you don't love and more of what you do. Try new foods like taro and rabbit. Try new exercises like tai-chi and crossfit. Challenge yourself by learning new things like surfing, bungee jumping or playing guitar. Spend more time doing the things you love with your loved ones, family, nature and animals.

Step 13: eat fat, saturated and mono saturated are best. Cook with duck fat, coconut oil and butter. Use olive oil, macadamia, or avocado oil in homemade sauces and dressings. Fat should be your friend, your body and higher levels of energy will thank you for it.

Step 14: drink a lot of water. Drink water when you feel a craving, it will keep you full and stop you from straying the wrong way.

Step 15: make time for meal prep. You should spend your free time on weekends prepping all your meals for the week. This will keep you from eating the wrong things after a long day at work, and when you are too tired to cook the right kind of meal.

Shopping Guide for the Paleo Diet

You have already set yourself up to stick to the Paleo diet, but then you go to the grocery store and you are surrounded by aisle after aisle of grains, processed foods, sugar and who knows what else. These foods are relatively easy to avoid because they are not part of the paleo diet, but some of the so called 'healthy foods' that are marketed can come off as confusing. So how do you know what to get from the grocery store? Here is a simple shopping list for the Paleo diet. It is a comprehensive food list for the Paleo diet with the vegetables, meats, oils, seeds, nuts and fruits that you are allowed to eat, and there are even some desserts. This list will provide you with a solid starting point for the Paleo diet.

Here is a basic reminder of the foods that are allowed:

Paleo diet meats, Paleo diet vegetables, Paleo diet fruits, Paleo diet oils/fats and Paleo diet nuts.

These are the foods that are not allowed:

Dairy, fruit juices, soft drinks, sweets, starchy vegetables, salty foods, grains, fatty meats, legumes and starchy vegetables.

- **Paleo Diet Meats**

   Nearly all meats are Paleo by definition, but of course, you want to stay clear of very processed meats and meats that are too high in fat, like hot dogs, spam and other meats that are low quality. If it used to oink, moo, or make any type of sound then it is certainly Paleo. Poultry, shrimp, turkey, lamb rack, chicken breast, chicken wings, pork tenderloin, chicken leg, pork chops, chicken thigh, steak, grass fed beef, bacon, ground beef and pork are all viable options for you. Eggs (chicken, goose, or duck), lobster, bacon, clams, bear, venison steaks, goat, buffalo, rabbit, New York steak, and lamb steak are good too.

- **Paleo Diet Vegetables**

   Nearly all vegetables are viable for the Paleo diet too but you should be cautious when determining the difference. Vegetables that have a high starch content like squashes and potatoes have a tendency to have low nutritional value when compared to how much sugars, carbs and starches they contain. They are not bad for you but they are not always good for you either.

   Asparagus, green onions, avocado, eggplant, artichoke hearts, parsley, Brussel sprouts, cauliflower, carrots, peppers, spinach, cabbage, celery, zucchini and broccoli are all acceptable as well as beets, butternut squash, sweet potato, acorn squash and yams.

- **Paleo Diet Fats/Oils**

  Contrary to popular fat, fat does not make you fat, carbs do and the diet you are currently on, the Standard American Diet has a ton of them. Natural fats and oils are the preferred method of your body for getting energy so it is best to give your body what it is asking for. Here are some of the best fats and oils for the Paleo diet that you can give your body and will help give you sustained energy. Grass fed butter, coconut oil, avocado oil and macadamia oil are good options. *awcOil*

- **Paleo Diet Nuts**

  Nuts are decidedly Paleo but be careful because peanuts and cashews have high levels of fat and they are too easy to eat in one sitting. If you are doing this to lose weight, you should limit the amount of nuts that you eat. These, however, are good to eat; almonds, walnuts, cashews, macadamia nuts, hazelnuts, sunflower seeds, pecans, pumpkin seeds and pine nuts are good options.

- **Paleo Diet Fruits**

  Paleo diet fruits are more than delicious, they are good for you as well. Fruits, even the ones approved for the Paleo diet, have high amounts of fructose, which may be better than high fructose corn syrup, but is still sugar. If you are trying to lose weight on the Paleo diet, you will want to cut back on how much fruit you eat and focus on the allowed vegetables for the Paleo diet. You can, however, have 1 to 3 servings of fruit every day, check out this list for the allowed fruits: apple, watermelon, avocado, strawberries, blackberries, lemon, papaya, grapes, peaches, blueberries, mangos, plums, bananas, pineapple guava, oranges, limes, raspberries, figs, tangerines and cantaloupes.

Here are some things to remember:

Starchy foods are good for energy replacement for those who are very active and spend a lot of time exercising, if this is you then you will need to eat starchier foods for energy sustenance as long as you are consistently exercising. But, if you are looking to lose weight on the Paleo diet then you will want to limit how much of those you are eating.

Eat high sugar fruits moderately, they are good for you but are easy to overdo. Keep in mind that you cavemen ancestors did not have access to Florida oranges so you do not want to be eating bowls and bowls of them while on this diet.

Eating Out on the Paleo Diet

I won't lie to you, eating out is very difficult while on this lifestyle. You may find yourself with very limited options and have to order off the menu to be sure you know what you are eating. But don't worry, it is all about awareness. It's not like you have a personal chef with you 24/7, in fact, 40% of the American population eat out at a restaurant at least once a week. You don't have to do it, but sometimes you have to, especially if you have friends and meet with family often. Here, you will find 18 tips for eating out like you are a Paleo pro.

1. Order in your mind before you go out- this take~~~~ *takes* more time and work but nearly all restaurant menus are online now, so just spend a few minutes before you leave to decide what you will order

2. Eat before you go to the restaurant- this is golden, it is socially awkward not to eat at a restaurant especially if you are out with friends but you don't want to end up starving if you know there isn't anything Paleo acceptable there for you to eat. This will make you less likely to order something that is unhealthy.

3. Try to go to certain types of restaurants- Mediterranean/Greek, Middle Eastern, steak and BBQ restaurants are great and offer plenty of Paleo choices.

4. National US chains are good- Chili's, Applebee's, TGI Fridays, and Outback have a good number of options to choose from like seafood, fajitas, chicken dishes

and steaks plus more. You will need to be sure to know what items are breaded or have sauces with added sugars.

5. Don't go to certain restaurants- you should still hang out with your friends even if it is not good for your diet but sometimes you should turn down some offers, especially to places like sandwich shops, pizza joints, Mexican restaurants and Italian restaurants.

6. Don't be shy to ask questions- you are the one paying for and eating the food so you have a right to know what is in it.

7. Pretend to have gluten allergies-gluten is of the worst things that you can eat at a restaurant but there really isn't a way around it. A lot of people are allergic to gluten and the restaurant does not want to be liable for getting anybody sick so if you tell the waitress you are allergic, they will make sure there isn't any in it.

8. Ask if the dish is breaded-this is especially good for seafood, you don't want to be shocked when you get a dish that is covered in breaded foods.

9. Tell them you are sensitive to something and allergic-sensitivities and allergies are not the same thing but they are similar enough, restaurants are a lot more careful with allergies so use it to your advantage.

10. Say you are on a prescribed diet-you do not have to give specifics, just give them the details that matter

like no processed sugar, no seed oils and no gluten. Most places will accommodate diets.

11. Ask about the cooking oil-it is hard to go nearly anywhere that does not cook with vegetable, canola or corn oil, this should be the first thing you ask.

12. Ask for olive oil as the cooking oil-until every restaurant has coconut oil, the best thing you can ask for is olive oil. Most restaurants already have it available.

13. Stay clear of added sugar-sugar is more than most times added at different stages of cooking and preparation so the wait staff might not even know. But you should ask.

14. Wait staff isn't all knowing, ask the chef-many of the tips aforementioned are good questions but the wait staff might not always know the answer, the chef normally will.

15. Substitute veggies as a side-vegetables may not be listed as an available side but most of the time, restaurants serve them as sides.

16. Ask for no MSG-if you are eating at an Asian restaurant, this is mostly for that but any other kind of restaurant might have it too, try to remember to ask as often as possible.

17. Ask the wait staff to leave tempting items off the table-like bread, if they try to put it there just say 'no

thank you, we don't eat bread.' Having it there just makes it much harder to resist.

18. Don't stress about it- if you are not really allergic to something, then don't worry about eating something that is not Paleo approved if it is not very often. Nothing can keep you from occasionally compromising your diet and that is ok, you can always do better on the next meal.

50 Paleo Recipes

Now that you know everything there is to know about Paleo, you need some Paleo dishes to actually eat. You don't have to be a qualified chef to pull off these recipes, they are easy to follow and fun to eat!

10 Paleo Breakfast Recipes

When you start your day the Paleo way, you will have more energy, feel less groggy and be more alert. You will even make it all the way to lunch without any pangs of hunger.

Banana nut Paleo pancakes
1 to 2 people

Ingredients

2 bananas, 2 tablespoons of chunky almond butter, 4 eggs, dark chocolate chips (optional)

Instructions

Mash bananas in a large bowl, combine the bananas with the almond butter and blend them with the eggs in a bowl. Mix it well and scoop out a quarter of the batter onto the hot griddle or pan over medium heat. Wait for it to bubble and then flip. Top the pancakes with dark chocolate chips if you want and serve.

Breakfast salad and eggs over easy
1 to 2 people

Ingredients

2 eggs, grass fed butter or coconut oil, fresh baby spinach, broccoli, avocado, onion, peppers and carrots and lettuce.

Instructions

Melt some of the coconut oil or grass fed butter in a small frying pan over medium to high heat. Crack 2 eggs inside and then cover it, prep your salad while you are waiting. Combine the spinach, onions, peppers, tomatoes, celery, broccoli, avocado and carrots then cook until your eggs are done how you like. You can season the salad with pepper and sea salt if you want, along with some olive or avocado oil if you want.

Breakfast smoothie
1 person

This is a very quick option if you are in a hurry.

Ingredients

Kale or spinach, frozen or fresh fruit, ice, additional vegetables.

Instructions

Add the kale or spinach in a blender, with the fruit, vegetables and ice. Blend until it is smooth. You can add some hard boiled eggs if you want.

No grain granola cereal
Yields 1-2 people

Ingredients

Paleo granola bars, almond, whole, or coconut milk

Instructions

Paleo granola bars are usually snacks, but if you are just dying for some cereal, break apart the bars in a bowl and use almond, whole, or coconut milk.

Leftovers
Yield varies

Ingredients

Whatever you had last night for dinner or lunch

Instructions

One of the best satiating and hearty breakfasts that gets overlooked are your leftovers. We tend to get stuck in thee norm of waffles, cereal or eggs being our only breakfast options. All you have to do is look in your fridge for some beef, chicken or pork and add some vegetables into a skillet and heat it up.

Avocado, peach, kale smoothie
1 person

Ingredients

½-1 avocado, ½ banana, 3-4 peach slices, ¼-1/2 cup of kale, about 1 cup of almond milk

Instructions

Mix the ingredients together in a blender. If you like sweeter smoothies, then add some honey.

Bacon stir fry
1-2 people

Ingredients

7-8 diced bacon slices, half a yellow onion, diced, 1 zucchini and
sweet
potato diced, 1 avocado and 7 beans, ground black pepper

Instructions

Cook the bacon in a skillet on medium to low heat, drain the fat
and then set the bacon aside. Heat a large sauté pan at medium
to high heat, add 11 tablespoon of bacon and the sweet potato
and onion. Stir well until the onions become translucent and the
potato is soft, then add the beans and zucchini then combine
the bacon and vegetables. Top with the ground pepper and
avocado.

Banana bites
1 person

Ingredients

1 banana, almond butter

Instructions

Slice the banana into round slices, around ¼ to ½ inch thick, then spread the desired amount of almond butter on one slice, then top it with another slice. Put them in the freezer for about half an hour. You can keep them in a sealed container for about a week.

Breakfast casserole
8-10 servings

Ingredients

1 pound of breakfast sausage, 10-12 large eggs, and 1 diced green onion, 1 large sweet potato, and 2-3 cups fresh baby spinach.

Instructions

Preheat the oven to 325 degrees and grease a baking dish with coconut oil. Prepare the vegetables, heat a skillet over medium to high heat and add the sausage, cook until browned. Remove the sausage but keep the grease, then add the sweet potatoes and cook until tender. Remove the sweet potatoes and place them in a bowl, toss them with the spinach, sausage, green onion, pepper and salt until it is combined. Place the mixture in the baking dish and spread evenly. In a separate bowl, whisk the eggs and pour the mixture over the sausage and vegetable mixture. Back in the oven for about 25 to 30 minutes. Cool slightly before serving.

reakfast egg muffins
Servings vary

Ingredients

1 tbs. olive oil, 1 large sweet onion chopped finely, 1 green pepper and red pepper chopped finely, 12 large eggs, ½ tsp. black pepper

Instructions

Preheat oven to 350 degrees Fahrenheit, sauté onions in olive oil over medium to high heat, add peppers and continue cooking for another 2 minutes. Whisk eggs in a large bowl, once the peppers and onions are cooked, remove them from the heat and let them cool. Add the onions and peppers to the bowl with the eggs and combine well with the salt and pepper. Coat a muffin pan with coconut oil or olive oil spray. Measure out ¼ cup of the mixture for each muffin cup. Bake for 10-15 minutes, or remove once the tops get high.

10 Paleo Lunch Recipes

Steak and eggs
1 person

Ingredients

1 large steak (sirloin, ribeye, filet), 2-3 tablespoons of your choice of cooking fat, 2 free range eggs, salt, pepper, and paprika.

Instructions

Heat a pan on medium to high heat and add 2 tbsp. of your choice of cooking fat. Season he steak with sea salt and fresh ground black pepper then add it to the hot pan. Cook the steak to your liking, remove the steak from the pan and set aside. Crack the eggs in the pan, cover, and then season with the paprika, pepper and salt until the whites set in. serve the steak with the eggs on top or on the side.

Paleo chicken fajitas
1-2 people

Ingredients

3 lbs. of chicken breasts cut into strips, 3 bell peppers, 3 onions, sliced, 2 tbsp. of oregano, cumin, chili powder and coriander, 6 chopped garlic cloves, juice from 5 lemons, 4 tbsp. of coconut oil, ghee or tallow and butter lettuce. Choose toppings like salsa, avocados, mayonnaise, guacamole, fermented pickles or diced tomatoes.

Instructions

Mix the chicken, onions, bell peppers, garlic, lemon juice and spices in a bowl and mix well. Heat a large skillet on medium to high heat and add the mix with the cooking fat until the chicken is cooked through and the peppers are soft. Put the preparation in a bowl and serve with lettuce leaves and toppings.

Liver and onions
1-2 people

Ingredients

4 large slices of beef or pork liver, 5 large sliced onions, salt and pepper, 6 tbsp. lard or butter.

Instructions

Heat a skillet over medium to low heat and add the butter and onions. Cook slowly and stir often for around 20-25 minutes until the onions are caramelized and soft. 5 minutes before the onions are done, heat a separate pan on medium to high heat to cook the liver with the rest of the cooking fat, around 3 minutes on each side. Serve the liver topped with the onions.

Bacon, spinach, and mushroom casserole
2-4 people

Ingredients

2 ½ lb. of good quality smoked bacon cut into medium strips, 3 handfuls of fresh spinach with the stems removed, 1 lb. of button mushrooms, 1 chopped large onion, 2 minced garlic cloves, 2 tbsp. of ghee, butter, or lard, salt and pepper.

Instructions

Heat all ingredients over medium heat and cook the bacon until it is soft, the garlic should be cooked until fragrant and the mushrooms cooked until soft. Season with pepper and salt and serve.

Baked salmon with asparagus and roasted beets
4 people

Ingredients

4 fresh wild salmon fillets, 4 tbsp. coconut oil or butter, 4 tsp chopped dill, 16 sprigs of asparagus, 4 medium red beets, 4 pcs of heavy duty foil, salt and pepper.

Instructions

Preheat the oven to 500 degrees Fahrenheit, place the beets and 4 asparagus spears on each of the four foil pieces then top them with the salmon filet. Add butter and dill on each fillet and close the foul. Bake in the oven for 10 minutes, be sure to check on it.

Chicken and zucchini hot salad
4 people

Ingredients

2 ½ lbs. chicken breast, 5 zucchinis, 3 tbsp. coconut oil, lard or ghee, 1 tbsp. oregano, 1 chopped large onion, 7 tbsp. mayonnaise, juice from 2 lemons, 2 cloves of garlic, 1 head of romaine lettuce shredded, salt and pepper.

Instructions

Heat a large pan on medium to high heat and cook the chicken cubes, then add the onion and cook until soft. Add the zucchini and oregano and season with the pepper and salt. In a bowl, mix the lemon juice, mayonnaise and garlic. Add the cooked chicken, zucchini and onion and mix well, then add the lettuce.

Sausages with mushrooms and parsnip mash
6 people

Ingredients

12 large pork or beef sausages, 2 lb. parsnip chopped, 2 tsp cooking fat, 5 tbsp. ghee or butter, 1 lb. button mushrooms, ½ cup fresh chopped oregano, pinch of nutmeg, pepper and salt.

Instructions

Boil the parsnips until soft, drain the water and add half the butter, nutmeg, salt, and pepper then mash well. You can use a food processor for this. Heat a large skillet on medium to high heat and cook the sausages for about 10 minutes with the cooking fat. Set the sausages aside and add the mushrooms with the other half of the butter and cook until browned, then add the chopped oregano. Serve with the mashed parsnips on the sausages with the mushrooms and all the drippings.

Canned salmon salad
2 people

Ingredients

2 cans wild salmon, 2 diced cucumbers, 1 chopped onion, 1 diced tomato, 1 diced avocado, 5-6 tbsp. of extra virgin olive oil, juice from 2 lemons, 2 tbsp. chopped fresh dill and lettuce leaves

Instructions

Drain the liquid from the canned salmon and place it in a bowl, mash it well with a fork, add the olive oil and lemon juice and mix well, add the onion, avocado, tomato and cucumbers and mix again, add the dill and season with pepper and salt and serve the cold salad on top of lettuce leaves.

White wine and garlic mussels
4 people

Ingredients

4 lbs. fresh mussels, 2 cups of white wine, 2 chopped onions, 5 chopped garlic cloves, 1/3 cup of fresh chopped herbs, 6 tbsp. ghee or butter.

Instructions

In a stockpot, combine the stock or wine, garlic and onions and bring to a boil, let it simmer for 5 minutes. Add the mussels and cover, then increase the heat to medium high so that the sauce can boil and create steam to cook the mussels. As soon as the mussels open, add the butter and herbs then remove from the heat. Serve with garlic, butter and wine sauce.

Pork chops with onions and apples
4 people

Ingredients

4 pork chops, 3 tbsp. ghee, coconut oil or lard, 2 large onions, 4 sliced and cored apples, salt and pepper.

Instructions

Heat a large pan on medium to high heat and season the chops with salt and pepper. Melt the cooking fat and fry the chops for about 5 minutes on each side, set the chops aside and reduce the heat, then add more cooking fat and add the apple and onion slices. Cook for 4 minutes until the onions have caramelized and the apple slices are soft, serve the chops topped with onions and apples.

20 Paleo Dinner Recipes

Ground beef stir fry
4 people

Ingredients

1 lb. of ground beef, 2 cups of stir fry vegetables, 2 tbsp. of garlic, ½ cup of onions, sea salt and fresh ground pepper.

Instructions

Brown the ground beef in a medium sized pan with the garlic and onions. Once the ground beef is brown add two cups of the vegetables and cook for 3-5 minutes, serve the dish hot.

Pan seared Cajun salmon
2 people

Ingredients

2.6 oz. of salmon filets, 1 tbsp. coconut oil, 1 tbsp. of cilantro, 1 tsp paprika, ½ tsp of oregano, ½ tsp of thyme, ¼ tsp of cayenne, ¼ tsp of garlic powder, ¼ tsp of onion power, ¼ tsp salt, 1/8 tsp of fresh ground pepper.

Instructions

Stir the ingredients together for the rub in a small bowl and rub into the salmon. Melt the coconut oil in a nonstick skillet on medium to high heat. Put the salmon in the pan and sear for 4 minutes until brown. Flip over and cook for 5 more minutes, serve warm with cilantro.

Vegetable curry

Ingredients

1 tbsp. of coconut oil, 2 tbsp. of curry paste, 1 diced yellow onion, 4 minced garlic cloves, ½ red bell pepper, ½ yellow bell pepper, 1 chopped yellow squash, 1 cut head of broccoli, 1 14 oz. can of coconut milk, salt, 2 tsp of lime juice, ¼ cup of cilantro

Instructions

Melt the coconut oil in a large pan and add the curry paste, cook for 3 minutes. Add the garlic and onions to the pan with salt, sauté for 5 minutes, and stir in the squash, broccoli and bell peppers, sauté for 3 more minutes. Add the coconut milk to the pan and let it simmer, cook for 15 minutes, adjust salt to taste, remove from heat and stir in lime juice. Top with cilantro to serve.

Salsa Verde chicken
4 people

Ingredients

2 lbs. of boneless chicken, 1 can of coconut milk, 2 cups of green Verde salsa, 1 tsp of salt, 1 tsp of onion powder, 1 tsp of garlic powder, 1 tsp of cumin, 2 tbsp. arrowroot powder.

Instructions

Preheat the oven to 400 degrees, add the ingredients besides the arrowroot to a large baking dish. Cover with foil and bake for 30 minutes. While it is baking, add arrowroot and water to a small jar, shake well. After 30 minutes, remove the chicken from the oven and add the arrowroot mixture then whisk into sauce, bake for 15 more minutes and serve over riced cauliflower or spinach.

Chicken salad
4 people

Ingredients

2 oz. of chicken breast, 3 hardboiled eggs, 1 tsp of garlic powder, 1 tsp. of onion powder, 1 tsp of salt, ¼ cup of sunflower seeds, ½ tsp cracked pepper, 1 celery stalk, 2 tbsp. of melted butter, sprinkle of dill.

Instructions

Chop and dice the eggs, grapes and celery, then mix them together in a bowl. Add the chicken breast, grapes and celery, then add the seasonings and sunflower seeds. Drizzle the melted butter over everything and mix lightly. Serve in lettuce leaves on a bed of fresh spinach.

Beef stew
6 people

Ingredients

1/5 lbs. of beef stew meat, 1 cup of onion, 3 tbsp. of minced garlic, 1 tbsp. of coconut oil, 8 oz. of sliced mushrooms, 2 tbsp. of grass fed butter, 1 tbsp. of balsamic vinegar, 1 inch of sweet potato chunks, 2 stems of diced celery, 1 bay leaf, 4 cups of beef broth, 2 tbsp. of arrowroot powder, 1 tsp of garlic powder and salt and pepper for taste.

Instructions

In a large oven, melt coconut oil and sauté the onions and garlic, prepare the meat by sprinkling sea salt, garlic powder and fresh cracked pepper on it, coat evenly on all sides. Heat up a second skillet to sear the meat, melt 1 tbsp. of butter in the skillet. Once the skillet is sizzling, add the meat and sear each side for 45 seconds, remove and add to the oven with the garlic and onions. Add 3 cups of the beef broth and turn the heat down to low, then add celery, bay leaf, and sweet potatoes to the oven. Using the pan that you used to sear the meat, warm the rest of the butter and add in the mushrooms, then put the arrowroot powder in a mason jar and fill it with the rest of the beef broth and shake until the powder is dissolved. Stir the mushrooms with vinegar and add the arrowroot and broth mix to the pan with the mushrooms, once the mushrooms and gravy have thickened, pour the contents in the oven with the soup. Bring the soup to simmer for 2 hours and stir occasionally.

Pie

2 lbs. of ground beef (grass fed), 4 minced garlic cloves, 1 medium chopped yellow onion, 2 chopped carrots, 1 container of sliced mushrooms, 1 bag of thawed frozen peas, 1 can of tomato paste, 2 lbs. of balsamic vinegar, 1 tbsp. of fresh rosemary, 2 tsp of fresh thyme, 4-6 sweet potatoes, ½ cup of coconut milk, 1 tbsp. of butter, sea salt and pepper.

Instructions

Preheat the oven to 350 degrees Fahrenheit. In a large skillet, cook the meat until it is browned with the butter and garlic cloves, after the meat browns, take it out of the pan and cook the carrots, mushrooms and onions until the onions are translucent and the carrots are soft. Add the meat back into the pan and then add the vinegar, salt, thyme and tomato paste, cook until the extra liquid is gone. Stir in the peas and pour the meat mix into a baking dish. Separately, bake the sweet potatoes in a foil lined baking sheet for about 40 minutes. Once cooked, let them cool before peeling them and put them in a medium sized bowl with butter, coconut milk, pepper and sea salt. Mash the potatoes into a paste and put atop the meat mixture, bake for about 20 minutes or until the sides bubble and the center is hot.

Spaghetti squash and meatballs
1-2 people

Ingredients

One medium spaghetti squash, one pound of Italian ground sausage, one 14 oz. tomato can, 2 tbsp. of hot pepper, 4-6 whole garlic cloves, 2 tbsp. of olive oil and Italian seasoning.

Instructions

Be sure to use a 6 quart slow cooker for this, put the tomato sauce, garlic, olive oil, Italian seasoning and hot pepper relish into the cooker and stir well. Cut the squash into half and scoop out the seeds then place them in the slow cooker. Roll the ground sausage into meatballs and fit as many as you can or want, cook on high for about 3 hours, or on low for 5. Use a large fork to pull the squash into 'spaghetti' and serve garnished with parsley if you want to.

Mini meatloaves
1-2 people

Ingredients

2 pounds of ground meat (grass fed, pork, or veal), 10 ounces of frozen chopped spinach, 1-2 teaspoons of oil, 1 diced medium onion, 6 ounces of diced mushrooms, 2 diced carrots, 4 lightly beaten eggs, 1/3 cup of coconut flour, 2 teaspoons of salt, 2 teaspoons of pepper, 2 teaspoons of onion powder, 1 teaspoon of garlic powder, 1 teaspoon of dried thyme and 1.4 teaspoon of grated nutmeg.

Instructions

Preheat the oven to 375 degrees Fahrenheit and that the spinach, squeeze out extra water and set aside. Heat a pan on medium to high heat and add the oil, fry the mushrooms and onions until the onions are translucent and the liquid has cooked out of the mushrooms then set aside to cool. Add the spinach, carrots, onions and mushrooms into a bowl with the ground meat, use your hands to mix it well. Fill regular size muffin pans to the top with the mixture and cook for about 30 minutes, allow to cool before serving.

Grilled pork chops and stone fruit slaw

4 people

Ingredients For the chops-

4 pork chops, 1 teaspoon of sea salt, 1 teaspoon of ground coriander, 1 teaspoon of ground cumin, 1 teaspoon of ground paprika. **For the slaw-**1 pound of assorted stone fruit (plums, peaches, apricots), ¼ teaspoon of ground chipotle powder, 1 teaspoon of lime zest, 1 teaspoon of lime juice and a pinch of sea salt.

Instructions

Preheat the grill on medium to high heat and combine the salt, coriander, paprika and salt in a bowl. Divide the rub among the chops and coat both sides, grill the chops for around 5 minutes on each side, remove to a plate and cover with lose foil for 10 minutes. While this is going on, prepare the slaw, add in the chipotle powder, lime zest and juice, and the salt. Serve the chops topped with the slaw or on the side.

Chicken tortilla soup
2 people

Ingredients

2 large chicken breasts with the skin removed, 1 can of diced tomatoes, 32 ounces of organic chicken broth, 1 sweet diced onion, 2 jalapenos without the seeds and diced, 2 cups of chopped celery, 1 bunch of chopped cilantro, 4 minced garlic cloves, 2 tablespoons of tomato paste, 1 teaspoon of chili powder, 1 teaspoon of cumin, fresh cracked pepper and sea salt, olive oil and 1 or 2 cups of water.

Instructions

In a crockpot over medium to high heat, add some olive oil and ¼ cup of the chicken broth, then add the onions, jalapeno, garlic, pepper and sea salt and cook until they are soft, add more broth if needed. Then add the remaining ingredients with enough water to fill the top of the crock pot. Cover and let it cook for around 2 hours. Once the chicken is cooked, it should shred easily. Top with cilantro and avocado slices to serve.

Hunter stew
2 people

Ingredients

2 lbs. of cubed beef, 2 handfuls of blueberries, and 2 cups of baby carrots sliced in half lengthwise, butter, coconut oil for frying, salt, oregano, pepper and garlic powder, 1 large sliced onion.

Instructions

Brown the beef in the coconut oil and simmer on medium with the onions until it softens up. Add in the seasoning to taste, add half a cup of red wine if you want and add enough water until the meat is covered. Add the berries in the last ten minutes with 1 teaspoon of butter, when the carrots are tender it is ready to serve.

Curry chicken stir fry
4 people

Ingredients

2 tablespoons of coconut oil, 1 16 oz. package of broccoli florets, 1 red bell pepper cut into strips, 1 cup of sliced onions, 3 tablespoons of minced garlic, 1 lb. of boneless, skinless chicken breasts cut into cubes, 1 tablespoon of smoked paprika, 1 tablespoon of red curry powder, hot sauce, cilantro, and red pepper flakes.

Instructions

Warm the coconut oil and cook the chicken strips in a large skillet on medium heat until the chicken browns, add in the broccoli, garlic and onions, steam on medium heat until tender for about 8 minutes. Add in the bell pepper and dry seasonings, stir to combine. Serve hot and add optional garnishes like red pepper flakes, cilantro or hot sauce.

Paleo fried fish sticks
4 people

Ingredients

1/2 lb. of trout, 2 eggs, 2 cups of almond flour seasoned with garlic and onion powder, salt, and pepper, 1.5 cups of coconut oil.

Instructions

Crack eggs into a bowl and whisk gently, put almond flour into a shallow dish and mix in the seasonings. Add the coconut oil to a pan on high heat, cut the fish into 2 inch strips and dip them in the egg batter then the flour, set them aside until the oil reaches a high temperature, it will be slightly smoky. Once it is ready, add several fish strips and fry each side for 2 minutes or until the flour is golden brown. Remove them once cooked and place on a plate lined with paper towels.

Grilled eggplant with pork and mint Bolognese
4 people

Ingredients

1 large eggplant, ½ lb. of ground pork, 1 can of tomatoes, 1 can of chopped mint, ½ cup of onions, 3 tablespoons of garlic, and 2 cups of mushrooms, 3 tablespoons sea salt and 1 tablespoon of coconut oil.

Instructions

Peel the skin off of the eggplant and cut it into discs about ¼ inch thick, then put it in a large serving bowl and coat them with the sea salt, set it aside for about an hour. While this is going on, add coconut oil to a large saucepan and sauté the garlic and onions until they are fragrant and translucent then add the ground pork and brown it. Once the meat as browned add in the mushrooms and onions then add the mint and mix it well. The eggplant should be good now, place it under cold water and rinse off the sea salt. Grill each side of the eggplant for around 7 minutes, once they are done lay 2 or 3 discs on each plate and add mint and pork Bolognese. Serve garnished with chopped mint.

Grilled salmon and zucchini
4 people

Ingredients

2 large thinly sliced zucchinis, 4 tablespoons of extra virgin olive oil, 2 teaspoons of kosher salt, ½ teaspoon of ground black pepper, 2 cloves of minced garlic, 1 whole salmon wild filet, 1/3 cup of fresh chopped basil, your choice of Paleo cooking spray.

Instructions

Preheat a grill to medium heat. Put the zucchini in a howl with 3 tablespoons of olive oil, 1 teaspoon of salt and ½ teaspoon of black pepper, toss evenly to coat the zucchini. Mash the garlic and ¾ teaspoon of salt on a cutting board and then put in a bowl and stir it in olive oil. Remove and bones from the salmon, coat a sheet of foil with cooking spray and put the salmon on the foil and spread the garlic measure over it, sprinkle the salmon with basil. Transfer the salmon onto the grill, cook for 12 minutes and then remove them to a cutting board, cut them into 4 equal portions. Grill the zucchini for about 6 minutes on each side, serve on a plate with some basil sprinkled on top.

Honey lime grilled chicken
4 people

Ingredients

2 halved boneless skinless chicken breasts, 2 tablespoons of lime juice, 1 tablespoon of apple cider vinegar, 1 tablespoon of honey, 1 teaspoon of coconut aminos, 1 minced garlic clove, ½ teaspoon of onion powder, ¼ teaspoon of black pepper.

Instructions

Put all of the ingredients besides the chicken into a small saucepan and stir over low heat until all the ingredients are blended well. Put the chicken breasts into a large Ziploc bag and pour the honey lime mixture over the chicken, close the bag and shake the chicken around so that it is coated well, refrigerate it for 30 minutes. Then, put the chicken on a hot grill and cook until it is done, serve with a side of vegetables or use for a salad.

Squash noodles with pesto
2 people

Ingredients

2 large zucchinis sliced, 1 large yellow squash, ½ cup of cherry tomatoes, 1 teaspoon of extra virgin olive oil, 1 clove of mince garlic, and a pinch of red pepper flakes, salt and paper, 2 cups of fresh spinach, juice of ½ lemon. **For the pesto-**1 cup of fresh basil leaves, 5 chopped garlic cloves, 3 tablespoons of pine nuts, juice from ½ a lemon, ¼ cup of extra virgin olive oil, /4 teaspoon of salt and fresh ground pepper.

Instructions

Slice the zucchini and squash into noodles with a peeler, line a colander with paper towels and put the squash there to drain for 10 minutes, meanwhile, toast the pine nuts in a skillet on medium to low heat, and stir frequently. To make the pesto combine all the ingredients in a blender and blend until fully combined, use salt and pepper for taste. Heat the olive oil in a skillet on medium to high heat, then add in the red pepper and garlic flakes, sauté for around 1 minute, add the squash and sauté for 4 minutes, stir in the spinach and pesto. Cook until the spinach is wilted, remove from the heat and stir in the tomatoes, drizzle with lemon juice and top with pine nuts. Serve immediately.

Taco salad

2 people

Ingredients

1 head of romaine lettuce, 2 roma tomatoes, ¼ red onion, ¼ cup of black olives, 1 avocado and 1 tablespoon of cilantro. **For the meat-**1 pound of ground beef, 2 teaspoons of chili powder, 1 teaspoon of cumin, ½ teaspoon of paprika, ½ teaspoon of garlic powder, ¼ teaspoon of onion powder, ¼ teaspoon of oregano, fresh ground pepper and salt.

Instructions

Put the tomatoes, lettuce, olives and onions into a large bowl and toss to combine, brown the ground beef in a large skillet on medium to high heat, stir in all of the spices and cook until the beef is not pink, stir regularly. Divide the lettuce among the plates and top with the ground beef mixture. Sprinkle with cilantro and avocado to serve.

Paleo vegetable curry

Ingredients

1 tablespoon of coconut oil, 2 tablespoons of panaeng curry paste, diced yellow onion, 4 cloves of minced garlic, ½ a sliced red bell pepper, 1 yellow squash, 1 broccoli head, 1 can of coconut milk, 1 teaspoon of coconut aminos, salt, 2 teaspoons of lime juice and ¼ cup of cilantro.

Instructions

Melt the coconut oil in a pan over medium heat, add the curry and cook for 3 minutes, add the garlic and onion with a dash of salt to the pan, stir frequently. Stir in the squash, broccoli and bell peppers then sauté for 3 more minutes. Add in the coconut milk and aminos and bring to a simmer. Cook for 15 minutes, adjust salt to taste then remove from heat and stir in the lime juice. Top with cilantro to serve.

10 Paleo Side Dishes/Snacks/Desserts

Perfect Paleo yogurt
2 people

Ingredients

1 can of coconut milk, 1 pack of gelatin, juice from 1 lime, 12 teaspoon of vanilla extract, 1 tablespoon of honey, raisins, cinnamon and honey.

Instructions

Set aside 1 cup of coconut milk and sprinkle with gelatin powder, then combine it well to make a creamy paste. Meanwhile, warm the coconut milk, stirring frequently to be sure it isn't too hot. Add the vanilla, honey, and lime juice to the coconut milk and combine well. Then, mix in the coconut milk paste and whisk constantly. Once combined, pour mixture into a dish and cover it and put it in the fridge for 1 hour or overnight. After you take it out, if it is more like jelly, put it in a blender with ½ cup of water to thin it out but if you like the jello consistency, go ahead and add the cinnamon, raisins and honey. Eat immediately.

Peaches and cream smoothie
2 people

Ingredients

2 ripe peeled, chopped peaches, 1 cup of coconut milk, a pinch of cinnamon, a dash of vanilla extract and 1 cup of ice.

Instructions

Combine all the ingredients into a blender and puree until it is smooth, add more coconut milk or ice and serve immediately.

Paleo mint brownies

4 people

Ingredients

1 cup of almond butter, 1/3 cup of honey, 1 egg, 2 tablespoons of coconut oil melted, 1 teaspoon of peppermint extract, ¼ cup of unsweetened cocoa powder, ½ teaspoon of baking soda, a pinch of salt and coconut oil spray.

Instructions

Preheat the oven to 325 degrees Fahrenheit, put the almond butter, egg, honey, peppermint and coconut oil into a large bowl. Use a hand blender to combine it until it is smooth. Mix in the baking soda, salt and cocoa powder. Prep a baking pan with coconut oil spray. Spoon the batter into the pan and bake for 20 minutes.

Apple crisps
4 people

Ingredients

2 diced apples, 3 tablespoons of butter, ½ cup of coconut milk and 2 tablespoons of cinnamon.

Instructions

In a warm saucepan, sauté the apples in butter for 3 minutes, turn the heat down and add in the cinnamon and milk, wait until the heat is reduced so that the milk does not curdle. Let it sauté for another 5 minutes and stir frequently, add to serving dishes and sprinkle with honey, sea salt and top with paleo granola.

Crunchy plantain chips
4 people

Ingredients

2 green plantains, juice from 1 lime, 1 tablespoon of coconut oil, sprinkle of garlic powder and sea salt.

Instructions

Preheat the oven to 400 degrees, slice and peel the plantains as thin as you can, add them to a parchment covered baking sheet. Drizzle with the coconut oil and lime juice, sprinkle with salt and seasonings to taste. Bake for 25 minutes and flip halfway through. Eat immediately or store in an airtight container.

Baked apples
4 people

Ingredients

5 apples cored, 2 tablespoons of walnuts, 2 tablespoons of pecans, 1 tablespoon of raisins, 2 tablespoons of grass fed butter, 2 teaspoons of cinnamon, ½ cup of apple cider.

Instructions

Mix the pecans, walnuts, cinnamon, butter and raisins in a large bowl. Fill the apples with the cut mixture and pack it in tight, pour the apple cider into a slow cooker, put it on low and cook for 8 hours.

Bacon wrapped Brussel sprouts
4 people

Ingredients

1 pound of Brussel sprouts, 1 pound of bacon and toothpicks.

Instructions

Preheat the oven to 400 degrees Fahrenheit, wrap each Brussel sprout with a half slice of bacon and secure with a toothpick. Place the wrapped sprouts on a baking sheet and cook for 20 minutes or until the bacon gets crispy. Serve immediately.

Pastrami wraps
2 people

Ingredients

4 ounces of pastrami, 1 head of lettuce, 8 teaspoons of brown mustard, 30 dill pickle chips, and ¼ sliced purple onion.

Instructions

Trim and rinse lettuce and lay out flat in sheets, place the pastrami pieces on each sheet of lettuce, top with the pickles, onions and brown mustard. Roll and secure with toothpicks.

Paleo chocolate chip cookies
1-2 people

Ingredients

1.5 cups of blanched almond flour, ¼ teaspoon of baking soda, ¼ teaspoon sea salt, 2 tablespoons of melted coconut oil, ½ teaspoon of vanilla extract, ¼ cup of maple syrup, 1 whole egg and ½ chocolate chips.

Instructions

Mix the dry ingredients together in a bowl the mix the wet ones in a separate bowl. Then, pour both together and mix well. Add in the chocolate chips and throw in the fridge to cool. Preheat the oven to 350 degrees Fahrenheit, spoon the batter onto a parchment lined cookie sheet, bake for 7 minutes, push on the cookies with a spatula then cook for 5 more. Let cool and serve.

Fried honey bananas
1 person

Ingredients

1 under ripe sliced banana, 1 tablespoon of honey, cinnamon, coconut oil or olive oil.

Instructions

Drizzle the olive oil in a skillet over medium heat, cook each side of the banana slices for 2 minutes. While this is going on, whisk the honey and 1 tablespoon of water, remove from heat and pour over the banana. Allow to cool and sprinkle with cinnamon.

Conclusion

By the time 2013 came around, the Paleo diet was the world's most widely known diet. But, it is still controversial among nutrition organizations and health professionals. Many have embraced the diet as reasonable and healthy while others believe that it is harmful. But, science can give us the real answers. There are 4 major points that have been comprised:

- We do not know exactly what our ancestors ate, so this diet is based on assumptions.
- This diet assumes that the body has not adapted to eating dairy and grains so these foods lead us to obesity, heart disease and more health problems.
- The average life expectancy of a caveman was around 20 years.
- The activity level for a caveman was much higher than ours is today.

  There are certainly very good benefits to the Paleo diet. It aids in weight loss and helps you make healthier food choices. It focuses on natural, unprocessed food choices and increasing the amount of produce you eat.

  There are many pros to this diet, it makes you feel good for one. You will feel like you have more energy and just feel lighter in general. This diet also offers a good set of principles that can lead you to a healthier diet, even if you don't stay with Paleo.

Free Ebook Offer

The Ultimate Guide To Vitamins

I'm very excited to be able to make this offer to you. This is a wonderful 10k word ebook that has been made available to you through my publisher, Valerian Press. As a health conscious person you should be well aware of the uses and health benefits of each of the vitamins that should make up our diet. This book gives you an easy to understand, scientific explanation of the vitamin followed by the recommended daily dosage. It then highlights all the important health benefits of each vitamin. A list of the best sources of each vitamin is provided and you are also given some actionable next steps for each vitamin to make sure you are utilizing the information!

As well as receiving the free ebooks you will also be sent a weekly stream of free ebooks, again from my publishing company Valerian Press. You can expect to receive at least a new, free ebook each and every week. Sometimes you might receive a massive 10 free books in a week!

All you need to do is simply type this link into your browser: http://bit.ly/18hmup4

About The Author

Hi, I'm Martin Rowland! Thanks for visiting my page, if you have read any of my books I sincerely hope they brought a lot of value into your life. If you haven't, what are you waiting for! A life full of health, energy and abundance await you, should you apply that you learn from my books. Clean Eating is my absolute passion, ever since I took the plunge a few years back my life has been phenomenal. I have competed in marathons, seen my abs for the very first time and completely transformed my mental health. When I meet people who haven't seen me since my transformation they are stunned. It's all down to clean eating.

Outside of writing and passionately preaching about clean diets I like to spend my time reading great fiction. I can often be found spending entire weekends sitting next to the lake beside my house engrossed in a novel. It has taken me a long time to get around to it, but I am finally enjoying the wonderful work that is George Martins' A Song of Ice and Fire series. Isn't it just brilliant? My other favourite thing to do is sailing. On the weekends where you can't find me beside the lake I will be cruising along the south coast on my wonderful yacht 'Poppy'.

Please get involved with my social media accounts, I try to keep the content inspiring or thought provoking.

Facebook - https://www.facebook.com/CleanFoodDiet

Valerian Press

At Valerian Press we have three key beliefs.

Providing outstanding value: We believe in enriching all of our customers' lives, doing everything we can to ensure the best experience.

Championing new talent: We believe in showcasing the worlds emerging talent by giving them the platform to grow.

Simplicity and efficiency: We understand how valuable your time is. Our products are stream-lined and consist only of what you want. You will find no fluff with us.

We hope you have enjoyed reading Martin's guide to the paleo diet.

We would love to offer you a regular supply of our free and discounted books. We cover a huge range of non-fiction genres; diet and cookbooks, health and fitness, alternative and holistic medicine, spirituality and plenty more. All you need to do is simply type this link into your web browser:
http://bit.ly/18hmup4

CPSIA information can be obtained
at www.ICGtesting.com
Printed in the USA
LVOW01s1517291115
464569LV00034B/1454/P